L. L. Owens

Contents

A Harcourt Achieve Imprint

www.Rigby.com
1-800-531-5015

What's Blowing in the Wind?

Picture the **wind**. OK, so maybe you can't really do that because you can't see the wind. But, you can imagine what the wind does. What do you see in your mind's eye? Do you see:

Ocean waves crash against the shore?
Autumn leaves drift across a park on a fall day?
A kite sail through the springtime air?
An umbrella turn inside out on a stormy day?
Your book report fly out the car window?

?

What do you think of when you imagine the wind?

What can the wind do for you? It can probably do more than you realize! The wind is a force of nature. It's part of the weather. The wind is around every day whether you realize it or not.

Think of all the ways you can use the wind. People have been using the power of the wind for thousands of years. How? Read on to learn more!

Chapter One
What Is Wind?

Let's start by taking a closer look at what wind is.
Put simply, wind is the natural movement of air. But what
causes the air to move and the winds to blow? Where does
the wind come from?

If you said that wind comes from the sun, you are
right! The sun creates wind as it warms the earth. Wind is all
about hot and cool air trading places with each other.

1. The sun's rays warm the land faster than the water.

2. Warm air over land rises.

3. Cool air over the water fills the space left behind.

First the sun's rays shine on the earth's surface. As land soaks up the rays, it gets warmer. The rays that hit water instead of land are **reflected**, or bent, back up. This warms the air and causes it to spread out and rise.

As the warm air rises, cooler air moves in. The cooler air fills the space that the warm air left behind. That movement of air is what we feel and what we know as wind.

The First Sailboats

The ancient Egyptians were among the first people to use the wind to get around. As early as 2800 B.C., they figured out how to add sails to their boats. These sails were made from the papyrus plant, which the Egyptians also used to make paper. Sailboats let people who had been rowing and paddling boats use the wind instead of their muscles. This meant that they did not have to work so hard to get from place to place.

These early sailboats saved people a lot of hard work. The sails on the boats made travel and trade much faster and easier, too.

Five thousand years ago, ancient Egyptians sailed boats called *dhows* down the Nile River.

Kites

On a windy day, it's fun to fly a kite! But did you know that kites also have a long history of other uses?

The Chinese used kites in battle more than two thousand years ago. They used the kites to send signals to their troops from long distances away. A high-flying kite could tell soldiers to attack, to move on, or to retreat.

Many scientists have also used kites. Wilbur and Orville Wright experimented with box kites. This helped them design the first working airplane in 1903.

Around the same time, Alexander Graham Bell, who invented the telephone, was also experimenting with kites and planes. He tried to build a box-shaped kite that could lift a person. Bell's first successful flight was in 1909.

The Wright brothers would pre-fly their airplanes as kites first, just to see if they would make it into the air.

What did Benjamin Franklin hope to prove when he flew his kite during a thunderstorm?

Benjamin Franklin is probably the most famous kite flier of all time. It is reported that in 1752 he flew a kite—with a metal key attached—during a thunderstorm. It might seem like a dangerous thing to do, but it was actually part of an important experiment.

When lightning struck the key, Franklin felt a shock. This proved that lightning contained electricity. This experiment never would have been possible without the wind that kept that kite in the air, ready for lightning to strike.

Chapter Two

What Is a Windmill?

You might think of the **windmill** as a tool for capturing wind power. But what exactly does a windmill do?

A windmill is a large, fan-shaped machine that turns wind into energy. It has large blades that catch the wind and spin. Windmills help people do what used to be backbreaking work. Through the ages, windmills have made life easier.

A few of the jobs windmills do are sawing wood, pumping water, and grinding grain. These are all things that used to be done entirely by hand.

Long ago, farmers used heavy millstones to crush grain to make flour.

For example, farmers need to crush grain to make the flour people use for bread and other foods. Before windmills were invented, people and animals did that job. To keep up with the demand for flour, someone had to turn heavy **millstones** all day, every day. A millstone is nothing more than a heavy wheel that the farmer rolled over the grain, crushing it into powder. It was hard work!

Imagine people and oxen pushing a handle that turned the millstone around and around in a never-ending circle. That task became so much easier once they figured out how to use the wind's energy to turn a millstone for them!

How Does a Windmill Work?

The windmill is an amazing machine. First the wind turns the blades, which are connected to a shaft, or pole. The shaft is connected to a machine that does the work. The turning blades spin the shaft, and the spinning shaft turns inside the machine.

A windmill can do more than just make electricity. It can grind grain, pump water, and saw lumber. It can also make paper and press oil from seeds. However, sometimes people build windmills just because they are so interesting to look at.

Tower mills such as this were specially-designed windmills with roofs that could turn so that the blades always faced the direction the wind was blowing.

13

Windmills in History

The earliest windmills were built between about 500–900 A.D. in Persia, which is now the country of Iran. Persians were the first people to build a simple windmill to grind wheat and barley.

The invention spread to China and throughout Asia. Windmills were common in these regions by the year 1100 A.D. During the 12th century, the French and English also started using windmills. Soon windmills could be found throughout Europe.

Spread of Windmills

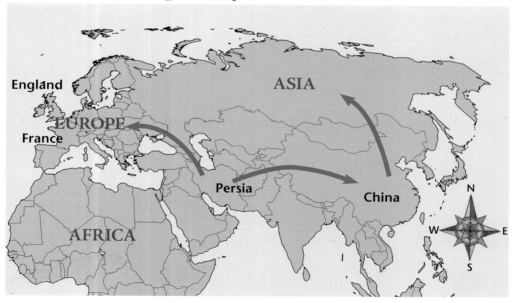

The use of windmills spread from Persia to the North and East during the 12th century.

The Netherlands is famous for its windmills.

The Dutch people living in the Netherlands covered their landscapes with windmills. They perfected the windmill design and used it to grind flour.

The most important job for the Dutch windmill was to drain the extra water from the land and pump it back out to sea. Most of the Netherlands sits below sea level, so the windmill really helped protect the land from flooding.

Between 1200 and 1900 A.D., the Dutch built about 10 thousand windmills! Fewer than 1,000 of them remain standing today.

Windmills also played an important role in the lives of the early American settlers. Settlers moved west looking for land. They also moved away from rivers and streams that were crowded with people to find pasture for their cattle. Often this land was very dry. From the 1800s until electricity made its way out to these communities, settlers in the American plains often used water-pumping windmills. These windmills worked well because the land is somewhat flat across the plains and the prairie. A flat landscape means that there are no tall trees or hills to block the wind.

What about the American plains and prairie makes it a great place to use windmills?

The settlers would dig down to the water that lay deep underground, then use the windmills to pump it up to the surface. That was the only way people could get to the water. Windmills helped early American farmers water their crops. They also helped farmers create a dependable water supply for their livestock and homes.

Because of the windmill, American farmers developed successful farming communities. Without the windmill, many farms would have been destroyed by **drought**.

Windmills in Art and Literature

The windmill was an important invention used by people of many cultures. So it should come as no surprise that the windmill appears in art and in literature as well.

The Dutch artist Jacob van Ruisdael painted beautiful landscapes. His famous work *The Mill at Wijk* captures the importance of the windmill in the Netherlands.

Ruisdael painted *The Mill at Wijk* in 1665.

In literature, J.R.R. Tolkien used the Sarehole Mill as a model for The Great Mill at Hobbiton in his famous series of books *The Lord of the Rings*. Sarehole Mill was one of Tolkien's favorite places during his childhood.

Henry Wadsworth Longfellow wrote a poem titled "The Windmill." In the poem, the windmill speaks directly to the reader and tells how proud it is of its work as a windmill.

The historic town of Pella, Iowa, is proud of its Dutch Mill. The windmill is a tourist attraction that helps visitors understand Pella's Dutch history. It is the tallest working windmill in the United States. When it was built in 2002, it was built to be taller than surrounding buildings and trees so it could capture the wind.

The mill in Pella, Iowa, grinds wheat into flour for the local bakeries and restaurants.

19

Wind Turbines

Many of the windmills built today are used to produce electric power. This power can be used to light and heat people's homes. These windmills are usually called wind **turbines**.

Like a regular windmill, a wind turbine has blades that turn when the wind hits them. They also have shafts that spin. Those turbines that are built on land are different than those built on the water. For example, because there is usually more wind over water than there is over land, wind turbines that are built offshore produce more electricity.

A wind turbine uses a giant **generator** to create electricity. Just like in a regular windmill, when the turbine spins from the force of the wind, it turns the shaft.

The shaft is connected to the generator. As the shaft spins inside the generator, the generator produces electricity. That electricity flows into power cables that supply businesses and homes with power. A one-**megawatt** wind turbine can give electricity to about 300 American homes.

Inside a Wind Turbine

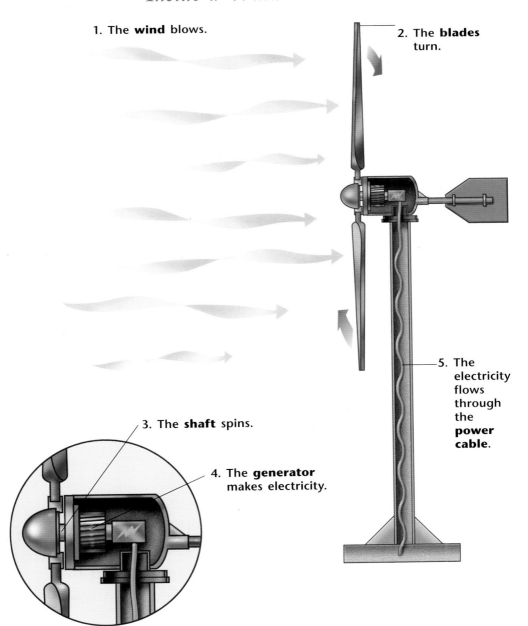

1. The **wind** blows.

2. The **blades** turn.

3. The **shaft** spins.

4. The **generator** makes electricity.

5. The electricity flows through the **power cable**.

Wind Farms

Have you ever heard of a wind farm? What do you think wind farmers grow? Why, wind, of course!

A wind farm is made up of a group of wind turbines. You might see just a few turbines in one place, or you might see thousands of wind turbines dotting the landscape. These turbines are usually owned and run by an energy development company.

At a wind farm, turbines stretch as far as the eye can see.

Sometimes a wind farm is the only thing on a stretch of land. Other times a wind farm is located on land that is used for other purposes. Some farmers let energy companies build wind farms on their land. In fact, you might see wind turbines standing tall, like modern scarecrows in the middle of a cornfield. You're most likely to find wind farms wherever the wind blows a lot, such as on open prairies, along coastlines, and on mountain passes.

23

Chapter Three

What is Wind Power?

During the 1970s, there was a time when the world didn't have enough gasoline and oil for everyone. This made gas and oil very expensive, and many people suffered. Some people in the United States could no longer afford to heat their homes or fill their cars with gas. And so when scientists began working to develop other energy sources, wind power seemed like a great idea.

When we flip a light switch, a light goes on. We don't usually think about where the electricity comes from to power the light. But, what would we do without electricity?

Much of our electricity comes from things like nuclear power and fossil fuels such as oil, coal, and natural gas. However, fossil fuels are nonrenewable. That is, they are found in small amounts under the earth. They can't last forever. These **resources** are being used up faster than they can be replaced.

Many people support the idea of building more electricity-generating wind farms. Why?

GAS SHORTAGE!
Sales Limited to
10 GALS. OF GAS.
PER CUSTOMER

During the 1970s, people waited in line for hours to fill up their cars at the gas pump. Prices were high, and gasoline was in short supply. If only cars could run on wind power!

Wind farms are very useful for generating electricity. But how dangerous are they for birds flying in the area?

The wind is a clean, natural energy source that will never go away. Nature will continue making wind as long as the sun warms the earth. **Environmentalists** call wind a renewable energy resource. They say it's important for our future.

People are becoming more interested in creating electricity through wind power. However, some people—and not just oil and **utility** companies—are fighting growth in the wind farm industry.

Some environmentalists worry that wind farms take up too much land. They also say that wind farms are noisy and that they disturb nearby wildlife. Worse, birds fly into the wind turbine blades and are hurt. In addition, wind turbines are expensive to build. This keeps many energy companies from building wind farms.

27

Which Way Does the Wind Blow?

Take a look at the good and bad sides, or the pros and cons, of the wind farm issue.

Wind Farm PROS

✖ **Wind is renewable.** Fossil fuels such as oil and natural gas will someday run out but there will always be more wind.

✖ **Wind doesn't pollute.** The burning of fossil fuels puts harmful chemicals into the environment. Wind farms generate electricity without pollution.

✖ **Wind is cheap!** Electricity produced by wind farms is less expensive than other sources. There are no fossil fuels to buy.

Wind Farm CONS

✖ **Wind is unpredictable.** Sometimes there is not enough wind, and sometimes there are strong storms that can damage the turbines.

✖ **Wind turbines are expensive to build.**

✖ **Wind farms use up lots of open land.** It takes plenty of open space to have a lot of turbines going. Plus, large wind farms can be noisy.

✖ **Wind farms can harm wildlife.** Birds can die when they fly into the wind turbine's blades.

The Future of Wind Power

We know we will always have wind, but we can't always tell what the wind will do. That is why wind power is not a perfect solution to our energy problems.

For example, wind speeds change from minute to minute, day to day, season to season, and year to year. When there is no wind, a wind turbine can't turn. And when there is more wind than expected, a wind farm can end up with more electricity than it can use.

People put weather vanes on roofs to show which way the wind is blowing.

How will wind power help us in the future?

But, this doesn't stop people from building new wind farms all over the world. People are working with their governments, environmental groups, and energy companies to pre-plan for what will happen when we run out of fossil fuels. The goal is to address all the issues—both the good and the bad.

Today many people are working hard to protect the environment. They'll continue work on the development of wind power and other renewable energy resources.

What happens next, as they say, is written in the wind!

Glossary

drought a long period of dry weather when there is not enough rain to grow crops or refill water supplies

environmentalists people who work to help protect the natural world

generator a machine that turns motion into electricity

megawatt a measure of electricity, one million watts

millstones large, circular stones used to grind grain in a mill

reflect to throw or bend back from a surface

resource materials found in nature that people use

turbine a machine with blades that rotates when wind moves through it

wind the natural movement of air

windmill a machine that works when wind turns blades at the top of a tower

utility a public service, such as power or water